VIRGINIA

Maſſaw: (Maſſawomeck omecks

Signification of theſe markes.
To the croſſes hath bin diſcouered
what beyond is by relation.
Kings houſes
Ordinary houſes

MANN AHOACKS

The Saſquaſ ahanougs
are a Gyant like peo ple &
thus attyred

PEACK BAY

KVSKARA WA OKS

TOCK WOGHS

and halfe

Scale of Leagues

Leagues

Diſcouered and Diſcribed by Captayn John Smith 1606
Grauen by William Hole

Captain John Smith's
BIG AND BEAUTIFUL BAY

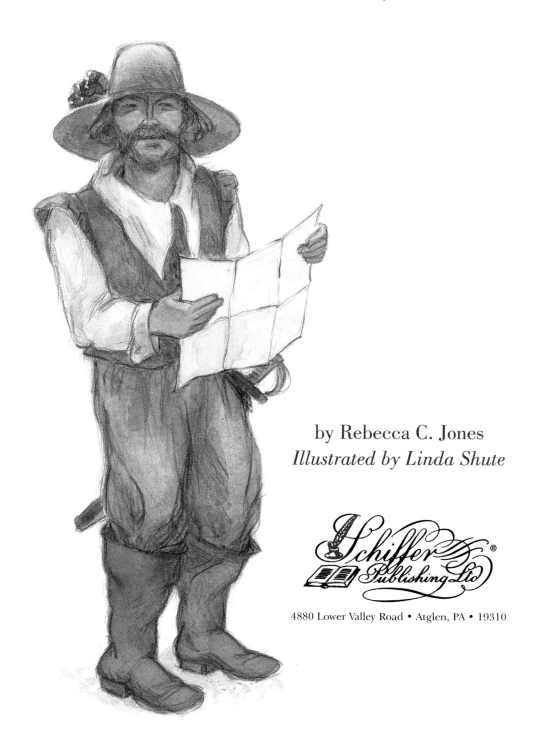

by Rebecca C. Jones
Illustrated by Linda Shute

Schiffer Publishing Ltd

4880 Lower Valley Road • Atglen, PA • 19310

To Jan Smith, a.k.a. Advice Lady
—R.C.J.

In loving memory of my husband, Dick, and
our days together on the bay and its rivers
—L.S.

Other Schiffer Books By The Author:
*The Mystery of Mary Surratt: The Plot to Kill
President Lincoln*, 978-0-87033-560-0, $9.95
The Biggest (and Best) Flag that Ever Flew,
978-0-87033-440-5, $8.95

Other Schiffer Books on Related Subjects:
*Finding Birds in the Chesapeake Marsh: A Child's
First Look*, 978-0-87033-533-4, $11.95
Olly's Treasure, 978-0-7643-3772-7, $16.99
Beddy Bye in the Bay, 978-0-7643-3450-4, $14.99

Library of Congress Control Number: 2011927149

Designed by **Danielle D. Farmer**
Cover Design by **Bruce Waters**
Type set in Bodoni Std./Braganza ITC/Corinthian

ISBN: 978-0-7643-3869-4
Printed in China

Schiffer Books are available at special discounts for
bulk purchases for sales promotions or premiums. Special
editions, including personalized covers, corporate imprints,
and excerpts can be created in large quantities for special
needs. For more information contact the publisher:

Published by Schiffer Publishing Ltd.
4880 Lower Valley Road
Atglen, PA 19310
Phone: (610) 593-1777; Fax: (610) 593-2002
E-mail: Info@schifferbooks.com

For the largest selection of fine reference books on this and
related subjects, please visit our website at
www.schifferbooks.com

We are always looking for people to write books on new
and related subjects. If you have an idea for a book, please
contact us at the above address.

This book may be purchased from the publisher.
Include $5.00 for shipping.
Please try your bookstore first.
You may write for a free catalog.

In Europe, Schiffer books are distributed by
Bushwood Books
6 Marksbury Ave.
Kew Gardens
Surrey TW9 4JF England
Phone: 44 (0) 20 8392 8585; Fax: 44 (0) 20 8392 9876
E-mail: info@bushwoodbooks.co.uk
Website: www.bushwoodbooks.co.uk

Captain John Smith's
BIG AND BEAUTIFUL BAY

Ring-billed Gull   Caspian Tern

More than four centuries ago, 144 Englishmen came to the New World. They pitched tents and built a crude fort in a place they called Jamestown. They didn't know it then, but they were planting seeds for a new country—the United States of America.

Most of the Jamestown men didn't care about starting a new country. They just wanted to find gold and become rich. They dug for gold in the ground around Jamestown, and they looked for gold in the nearby James River.

One man, though, didn't care about finding gold. Captain John Smith was much more interested in exploring this New World. He had so many questions: What kind of people lived here? What kind of animals? What kind of crops would grow here? And where do the rivers lead?

Most of the Jamestown men thought: Who cares? They just wanted to find gold and return to England. They wished John Smith would go away.

Finally, he did.

I THINK HE'S HEADED OUR WAY.

Great Blue Heron

Captain Smith explored the woods around Jamestown, and he followed the James River as far as it went. But he wanted to see more. He wanted to explore the big and beautiful bay called the Chesapeake.

WHY IS IT CALLED CHESAPEAKE?

NATIVE PEOPLE GAVE IT THE NAME CHESEPIOOC, WHICH MEANS "GREAT SHELLFISH BAY."

GREAT NAME!

Hard Clams

Eastern Oysters

Captain Smith had heard stories about the beautiful Chesapeake and the mighty rivers that flowed into it. He wondered whether those rivers flowed all the way from the South Sea—what we now call the Pacific Ocean.

Explorers had been looking for a water route between the Atlantic and Pacific oceans for more than a century. Maybe the Chesapeake Bay was the route they needed. The only way to know for sure was to go out on the bay and see where it led.

WHY DO EXPLORERS THINK THE CHESAPEAKE MIGHT CONNECT THE OCEANS? DON'T THEY REALIZE HOW BIG AMERICA IS AND HOW MANY MOUNTAINS AND PRAIRIES IT HAS?

UH. NO. THEY'VE NEVER BEEN TO AMERICA BEFORE. THAT'S WHY THEY'RE CALLED EXPLORERS.

Little Blue Heron

Snowy Egret

William Cantrill
Gentleman

Richard Featherston
Gentleman

Jonas Profit
fisherman, sailor

James Bourne
Gentleman

James Watkins
laborer, soldier

Anas Todkill
Soldier

Thomas Momford
Gentleman

Walter Russell
Physician

John Powell
tailor, sail maker

Robert Small
carpenter, boat repairman

Ralfe Murton
Gentleman

James Read
Blacksmith

Michell Sicklemore
Gentleman

Richard Keale
fish merchant

Captain Smith picked fourteen men to join him in the adventure. He chose men who were willing to work—and willing to give up the search for gold for a few weeks. He made sure to include a doctor, a carpenter, a blacksmith, a tailor, several former soldiers, a fisherman, and a fish merchant. He expected to find a lot of fish in the bay, and he wanted to identify them all.

The men put together a small but sturdy wooden boat, called a shallop. It had no cabin or roof to protect the crew from gusting winds, drenching rains, or blazing sun. The shallop was completely open.

Captain Smith put a compass and writing materials in the shallop, so he could draw accurate maps and take extensive notes. He also packed beads, bells, and other gifts for the native people he expected to meet along the way.

The men filled several barrels with fresh drinking water and packed enough bread to last the entire trip. For some reason, they did not pack any poles or nets to catch the fish they expected to find.

After loading everything, the men saw how crowded the small boat would be. They realized they would have to sleep sitting up because there was not enough room to lie down.

WHY CAN'T THEY ROW TO SHORE AND SLEEP ON THE GROUND AT NIGHT?

CAPTAIN SMITH DOESN'T KNOW WHO OR WHAT MIGHT BE ON THOSE SHORES.

I DON'T LIKE BEING ON LAND, EITHER.

Horseshoe Crab   Sea Nettle   Spadefish

On June 2, 1608, they left Jamestown. The shallop followed a supply ship bound for England down the river to the Chesapeake Bay. When the big ship headed out to the Atlantic Ocean, the little shallop turned into the bay.

Ahead, the bay's blue water sparkled like sapphires.

When the men looked up, they saw seagulls, herons, ducks, geese, and eagles flying in the sky. When they looked to the shore, they saw deep and dark woods.

ABOUT 300 DIFFERENT SPECIES OF FISH AND 30 DIFFERENT SPECIES OF WATERFOWL LIVE IN AND AROUND THE CHESAPEAKE.

American Avocet

When they looked down into the water, they saw more fish than they had ever seen before. Even the fisherman and the fish merchant were amazed.

Captain Smith said the fish were so thick that a man could walk across the bay on their backs. No one tried to do that, though.

I LIKE LIVING IN A DIVERSE NEIGHBORHOOD.

Lookdown Fish

In some places along the shoreline, people paddled out in canoes to greet Captain Smith. They invited him to bring his crew ashore for big feasts, with lots of dancing and singing.

In other places, people shot arrows and tried to scare Captain Smith away.

And in a few places, people shot arrows, and then invited Captain Smith and his men to come ashore for a big feast.

WHY ARE THEY CHANGING THEIR MINDS?

MAYBE THEY LIKE THE GIFTS CAPTAIN SMITH BRINGS THEM.

OR MAYBE THEY'RE AFRAID OF THE GUNS HE CARRIES.

Sanderlings

Black-Crowned Night-Heron

Captain Smith and his crew did not stay anywhere long. Steering by stars and by compass, they explored the twists and turns of the shoreline. Captain Smith was sketching a detailed map of their journey, and he wrote down everything that happened along the way.

Several times the shallop was in terrible storms. Once fierce winds broke its mast and swept a sail overboard. The crew frantically bailed water out of their boat. They kept it afloat long enough to reach a small island.

The storm lasted two days. While waiting for it to end, the men built a new mast and used their shirts to mend the sail.

When the sun came out, they were ready to continue their journey.

LET'S GO, BOYS! THE CHESAPEAKE AND ITS RIVERS HAVE MORE THAN 11,000 MILES OF SHORELINE, SO WE'VE GOT LOTS OF GROUND TO COVER.

Rainbow Snake

It was a hard journey. Even when the weather was calm and no one was attacking, the shallop rocked constantly with the motion of the bay. Water sloshed on everything and everyone. The bread grew stale, but got wet so often that it turned green with mold.

The men ate the green bread, but longed for better food. They also longed for dry clothes, an end to the shallop's motion, and a chance to lie down at night. They feared this journey—and the bay itself—would never end. They begged Captain Smith to turn the shallop around and return to Jamestown, before they were lost forever.

Captain Smith reminded the men that he was sharing their work and their misery (and their green bread). He asked them to have faith in him and enjoy the adventure. But the men didn't have faith, and they were tired of adventure. So Captain Smith agreed to turn back toward Jamestown.

Kingfisher

Osprey

Laughing Gull

On their way back, they came across a wide river called the Patawomek. (It's now known as the Potomac River.) Captain Smith estimated that the river's mouth—where it met the Chesapeake—was nine miles wide. Here at last, he thought, was the river that would lead to the great western ocean.

Even the tired crew was excited and wanted to sail up the river. The men became even more excited when they spotted a stream that sparkled with shining flecks. They were sure the flecks were silver or maybe even gold, and they imagined how rich they would all be.

The men rowed ashore and followed the sparkling stream through the woods until they came upon piles of glistening sand. They filled several bags with sand and carried them to the shallop.

Then they headed back toward the Chesapeake Bay.

DO THE BAGS REALLY CONTAIN SILVER OR GOLD? WILL THE MEN GET RICH?

NO. WHEN CAPTAIN SMITH SENDS THE BAGS TO LONDON, HE'LL LEARN THEY CONTAIN NOTHING MORE THAN PRETTY DIRT.

River Otter

Beaver

The men were still hungry—and frustrated that they didn't have a net or pole to catch some of the fish swimming around their boat. They tried to scoop fish out of the water with a frying pan, but that didn't work. The fish just scattered and swam away.

Captain Smith decided to try something different. He drew his sword and began to stab fish. The other men did the same thing, and within an hour, they had enough fish for everyone to eat.

As Captain Smith was sliding the last fish off his sword, he felt a sharp pain. He had caught a stingray, and its tail was shooting poisonous venom into his wrist. Soon his arm swelled to twice its normal size.

Everyone—including John Smith himself—was sure he would die. He directed the crew to row ashore, and he picked a spot for his grave. The men began digging.

But the crew's doctor did not give up. He heated a "precious oil" and smeared it on Captain Smith's arm. Soon the swelling went down. By that evening, the captain was well enough to eat the stingray that had attacked him.

THE PLACE WHERE THIS HAPPENED IS STILL CALLED STINGRAY POINT.

Cownose Ray

Captain Smith knew he needed a surgeon to cut the poisonous venom out of his arm, so the shallop returned to Jamestown. He stayed only three days—just long enough to have the surgery and to be elected president of the colony. With his arm still in bandages, Captain Smith returned to the big and beautiful bay.

WHY IS HE IN SUCH A HURRY?

HE WANTS TO FINISH EXPLORING THE BAY BEFORE HE TAKES OFFICE AS PRESIDENT.

Diamondback Terrapin   Bald Eagle

This time Captain Smith took a somewhat different crew. He picked twelve men, including some from his old crew and some who had missed the first trip.

ANTHONY BAGNALL
Physician

WILLIAM WARD
Tailor of clothes,
tarps and sails

NATHANIEL POWELL
Gentleman

EDWARD PISING
Carpenter and
Boat Repairman

NEW CREWMEN   JULY 24, 1608

Two days after the shallop left Jamestown, eight men got sick. They held their bellies and groaned with fever as they leaned and lay against the sides and bottom of the boat.

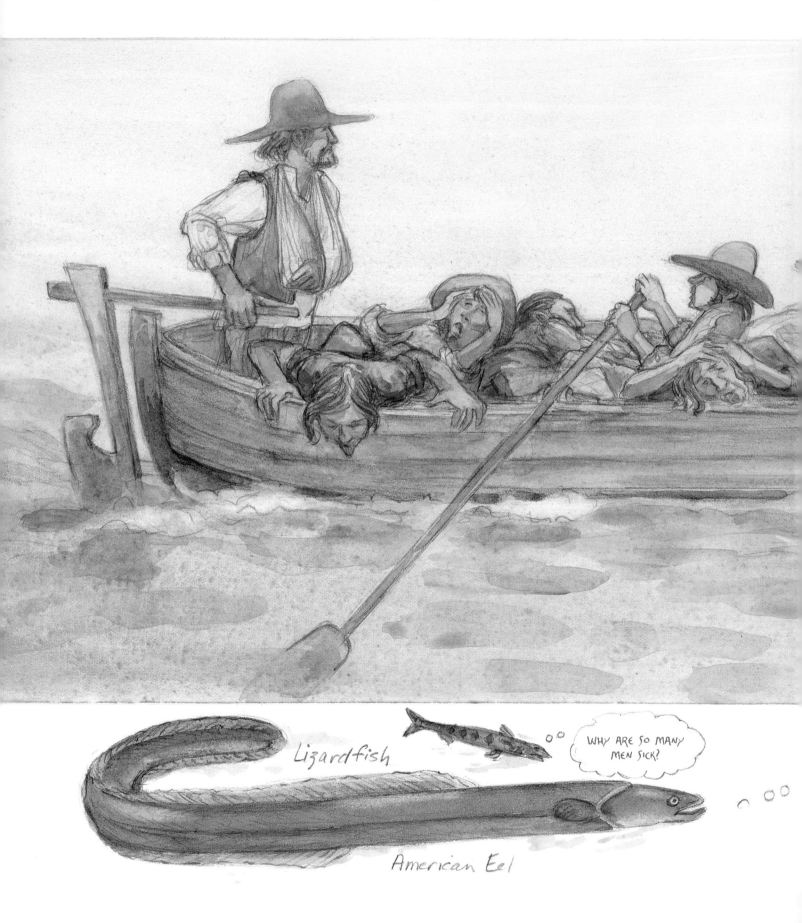

Even with most of his crew unable to row or work the sails, Captain Smith did not turn back. He headed for the far end of the Chesapeake, so he could continue to explore the big and beautiful bay.

THEY ARRIVED ON THE MOST RECENT SHIP FROM ENGLAND. MOST ENGLISHMEN GO THROUGH A PERIOD OF SICKNESS WHILE THEY GET USED TO THE WATER, FOOD, AND WEATHER IN THE NEW WORLD.

I JUST HOPE THEY STAY AWAY FROM ME.

Northern Puffer

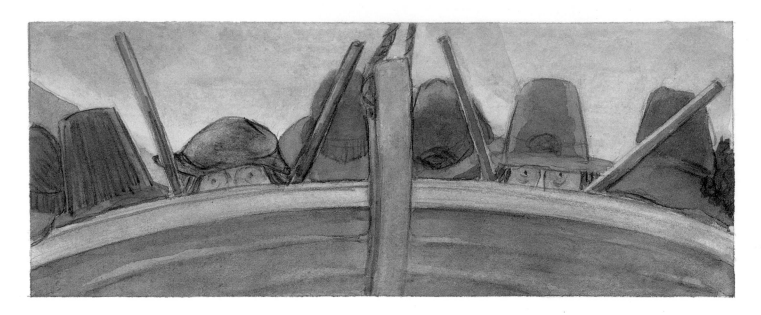

One morning Captain Smith spotted eight large canoes, filled with armed warriors, heading toward the shallop. They carried knives, spears, bows, and arrows—and looked like they were ready to attack.

Captain Smith knew that his crew, with so many men sick, wouldn't be able to defend themselves. But he did not try to escape.

Instead, he pulled a tarpaulin, or heavy cloth, over the sick men and gathered up their hats and guns. He propped those empty hats and guns along the side of the shallop. Then he raised the sail and headed straight for the warriors' canoes.

When they saw what looked like a well-armed boat coming straight at them, the warriors turned their canoes around and headed for shore.

Wild Turkey   Baltimore Oriole

Following Captain Smith

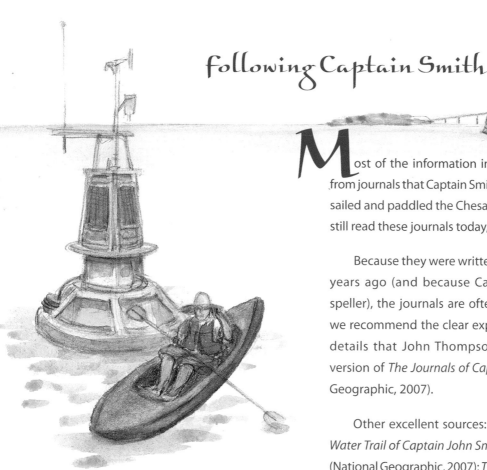

Most of the information in this book comes directly from journals that Captain Smith and his crew kept as they sailed and paddled the Chesapeake Bay in 1608. You can still read these journals today, both in print and online.

Because they were written more than four hundred years ago (and because Captain Smith was a lousy speller), the journals are often hard to understand. So we recommend the clear explanations and fascinating details that John Thompson provides in his edited version of *The Journals of Captain John Smith* (National Geographic, 2007).

Other excellent sources: *Chesapeake: Exploring the Water Trail of Captain John Smith* by John Page Williams (National Geographic, 2007); *The Great Rogue: A Biography of Captain John Smith* by Paul Lewis (David McKay Co., 1966); *John Smith's Chesapeake Voyages, 1607-1609* by Helen C. Rountree, Wayne E. Clark, and Kent Mountford (University of Virginia Press, 2007); and *The Three Worlds of Captain John Smith* by Philip L. Barbour (Houghton Mifflin, 1964).

Several websites describe Captain Smith's adventures on the Chesapeake. We particularly recommend two that track his explorations: www.johnsmith400.org and www.nationalgeographic.com/chesapeake. We also recommend visiting Historic Jamestowne (the site of the original Jamestown colony) and the reconstructed Jamestown Settlement, both near Williamsburg, Virginia.

If you'd like a wetter experience (and if you have access to a boat on the Chesapeake Bay), you can follow the crew's watery path, which is marked by big yellow buoys on the Captain John Smith Chesapeake National Historic Trail. For more information, contact the National Park Service or see www.smithtrail.net and www.buoybay.org.

CAN WE GO ON THE WATER TRAIL?

SURE. HOP IN A BOAT, AND WATCH FOR THE BIG YELLOW BUOYS.

ACTUALLY, I TRY TO STAY OUT OF BOATS.

Spot fish

Rockfish or Striped Bass

Summer Flounder

Captain Smith continued to explore the Chesapeake for several more weeks. Altogether, he spent fourteen weeks on the bay and traveled more than two thousand miles in the summer of 1608. He found several major rivers, but he never found one that connected the Atlantic and Pacific oceans. (There is no such river.) And his men never found real gold or silver.

But he did return to Jamestown with careful notes and a remarkably accurate map of the Chesapeake and its rivers. His map looks different from today's maps because he drew the bay sideways, rather than up and down. Even so, John Smith's map is so accurate that ship captains, settlers, and sailors used it for the next 300 years.

In 1609 Captain Smith went back to England and never returned to the New World. For the rest of his life, though, he praised the big and beautiful Chesapeake Bay. He believed the land around it would grow into a great nation someday.

That's exactly what happened. The land stretched beyond the Chesapeake, across forests and mountains and prairies and deserts, all the way to the Pacific Ocean and beyond. It became the United States of America.